The Tiny Museums

Carolyn Abbs

Carolyn Abbs grew up in a seaside town in the south of England and now lives by the sea in South Fremantle, Western Australia. She has a PhD from Murdoch University where she taught literature in the School of Arts for a number of years. *The Tiny Museums* is her first collection of poetry.

Other titles in the UWAP Poetry series (established 2016)

Our Lady of the Fence Post by J. H. Crone

Border Security by Bruce Dawe

Melbourne Journal by Alan Loney

Star Struck by David McCooey

Dark Convicts by Judy Johnson

Rallying by Quinn Eades

Flute of Milk by Susan Fealy

A Personal History of Vision by Luke Fischer

Snake Like Charms by Amanda Joy

Charlie Twirl by Alan Gould

Afloat in Light by David Adès

Communists Like Us by John Falzon

Hush by Dominique Hecq

Preparations for Departure by Nathanael O'Reilly

Chromatic by Paul Munden

The Criminal Re-Register by Ross Gibson

Fingertip of the Tongue by Sarah Rice

Carolyn Abbs
The Tiny Museums

Photographs by
Elizabeth Roberts

First published in 2017 by
UWA Publishing
Crawley, Western Australia 6009
www.uwap.uwa.edu.au

UWAP is an imprint of UWA Publishing
a division of The University of Western Australia

This book is copyright. Apart from any fair dealing for the
purpose of private study, research, criticism or review, as
permitted under the *Copyright Act 1968*, no part may be
reproduced by any process without written permission.
Enquiries should be made to the publisher.

Copyright © Carolyn Abbs 2017
The moral right of the author has been asserted.

National Library of Australia
Cataloguing-in-Publication entry:
Abbs, Carolyn, author.
The tiny museums / Carolyn Abbs.
ISBN: 9781742589541 (paperback)
Grief—Poetry
Australian Poetry—21st century.

Designed by Becky Chilcott, Chil3
Typeset in Lyon Text by Lasertype
Printed by Lightning Source

This project has been assisted by the Australian Government
through the Australia Council, its arts funding and advisory body.

This project is supported by the Copyright Agency Cultural Fund.

 uwapublishing

For my parents, Alexander (Alec) and Betty McClair

Contents

Part One 11
The Silver Bracelet 13
Knitting 14
First Memory 15
Tish Tosh Dress 17
Seaweed 18
Making Do 19
Drops of Blue Rain 20
First Voices 21
Tobacco Leaves 22
Degas Dancer 23
Doll 24
Shoes 25
Bognor Regis, 1962 26
Dead Bells 27
To the Lake 29
Triple Mirrors 30

Part Two 31
At the House where my Father was Born 33
Walls Haunt Me – in two voices 35
A Day in April, 1939 43
Alexander (late 1939) 45
In Hilda's Garden 46
Swallows 47
Piece of Lace 48
Never Trust Tulips 49
Tulips in Black and White 50

Part Three 51
Postcard to a Sibling 53
Because He Tried So Hard 55
Not Thinking it would be Forever 56
The Shrine 58
Sisters 59
After *The Secret Garden* 61
The Mulberry Tree (circa. 1600) 62
Anemones (black & white) 63
Above a Seedy Bridal Shop 64
Victorian Ring 65
Miss Philipou's Class 66
Sister Anne-Marie 67
Marilla 68
The Boy from the Grammar School 69
Three Pictures 70
An Attic Window (Montmartre) 72
Rural Normandy 73

Part Four 75
Surely Someone 77
No-one Knew 78
Für Das Kind 79
London, 1975 80
Apartment in Amsterdam 82
Bony Fingers 83
Dressing Gown 84
Alice 85
A Photographic Portrait 86
Doris Lessing, 1959 87
Girl at Bus Stop 88
Poet on Train 89
Well-thumbed Corner 90
On (mis)remembering a Bill Viola video installation 91
Jetlag at the Kelvingrove 92
Merchant Hall (York) 93
Monet's Room 94
Mona Lisa 95

Part Five 97
Sea Houses 99
A Black Swan 100
Ward One, Shenton Park 101

Age Sixteen 102
Orphan's Boot 104
The Pain of Faces 105
Famine 106
Decisively 107
Man with Dog on a Bench 108
The Cat in the Courtyard 109
Following, Watching 110
Cabbage White 111
Gone 112
Kaleidoscopic Pages 113
An Old Map 114
Tops of Norfolk Pines 115
Eden Way 116
Alistair 118
Baby Dress 119
First Steps 120
Slow Walk Home 121

Acknowledgements 123

Part One

The Silver Bracelet

Poetry attempts a dialogue with the departed,
Simon Armitage

My mother hid the bracelet
between folds of silk in her underwear drawer:
each oval disk the size of a finger-tip, petal smooth
beneath, embossed on top with black Indian elephants;
disks linked with fine chain, the way elephants trail
trunk to tail   the clasp broken,
missing

and all those years, I sensed the sadness
the sorrow, perhaps death, who knows.
Something to do with the war...
Her voice lingers in my poem, leaving
the same question
that as a child, I knew   not to ask.

Knitting

when she knitted   she sat forward in the chair
ready to leap up   listening   for cries from the pram –
the pattern spread on her lap: matinee coats
bonnets   bootees –   she counted stitches   whispered
complications of knitting.

fetch Rosebud   *Diana*   or *Dulcie*   she'd say –
I trailed dolls along the lino floor   to be measured
and afterwards   hurled them   into their cot.

each day   at a quarter to two
I climbed on her chair   switched on the radio
    are you sitting comfortably?
I settled beside her   waited   for the story to begin,
the knitting   at her feet.

First Memory

...there she was from the very first.
Virginia Woolf, Moments of Being

i.
it was just her　　and me:
hush　　her voice　　an echo in a cold room –
floorboards　　dusty　　my dress
was white　　she swept the curtain across –
April sunlight
　　　　　　　on the metal side of a pram –
huge wheels　　turned　　*tick　　tick* –
must not put my fingers in the spokes –
she lifted me　　to see,
i clutched the black hood　　concertina folds
up-down　　thwack　　umbrella sound,
i wanted to dive inside
but we left　　clunk　　the door was shut

she was gone

ii.
he took me outside　　a blue gate
　　　　　　　thin snow on the ground –
Look!　　a plane roared low in the sky
　　　　　　　metallic like a pram –
he held me tight　　i sobbed,
　　　wanted to go indoors　　to her –
the sleeve of his tweed jacket scraped my legs
but his words　　soothed　　*there, there,*
the click of his pipe　　against his teeth,
　　　　　smell of tobacco　　his smell

a soft hankie   dried my face –
quietly   we went into the dark house,
i sat on his lap
          she was in a bed across the room –
the midwife   wore a big white apron,
there was a trolley   a dark green cloth,
               instruments set out like cutlery –
go to her soon   soon –
she beckoned   and
               a newborn cried   in the crib

Tish Tosh Dress

silver taffeta
shot with pink   mauve   lemon
       lily-of-the valley-scent
the full-length skirt
    swished
           as she walked

Mummy, wear your tish tosh dress!

a strip of mirror
a key   my hand
involuntarily
    opens the door
listens
    for the tish tosh sound...
silence   mothballs
the chill   dark
    empty house after school

Seaweed
Fucus vesiculosus

She embroiders a seaweed pattern,
needle pricking satin, precisely (or thereabouts)
the tiniest dot, piercing, pulling taut   over and
over, forming fronds   knots: air-bladder blobs
children love to pop – cold touch, briny smell.

And there in her mind is the rush of the waves,
the breakwater, seaweed clings to rusty bolts
big as coat buttons – it's the olfactory that draws
her back to the school: girls making helluva din,
she descends stone steps to the cellar, clay floor,
rows of gabardine coats on pegs, walls steeped
in stench of the sea –
threading her arms through sleeves,
satin lining   dank as seaweed.

Making Do

My mother taught us tacking stitch,
back stitch, running stitch
and how to hem.
Learn to make do   she said.

I still see her:
mauve cross-over apron
leaning over the big oak table
in the cold front room, pinning
pieces of tissue dress pattern
to a remnant of curtain fabric;
cutting out with pinking shears.

At the sewing machine,
feet on the wrought iron treadle,
rocking back and forth, back and forth;
blonde head bent over her work;
one hand turning the wheel, the other
guiding fabric   peacock blue
silver thread spangling through.
She doesn't speak   pins in her mouth.

Drops of Blue Rain

chin high to Nana's ironing board,
I watch her place transfer paper

over fine white lawn, press and press
the iron, rows of dots appear like

drops of blue rain,
she sews running stitches in rows,

secures ends in figures of eight
around pins, gathers pleats, chooses

skeins of silk, embroiders rose, pale
mauve, blue, I raise my arms, squeeze

my eyes, the dress, prickly with pins,
slipped over my head, I am smoothed,

tugged, lifted high on a table,
turning as she measures the hem.

First Voices

You would wait in that dark room
for the dawn to create geometric shapes.

You would wait for each square, rectangle,
to mould a door, a wardrobe, a chair.

You would wait for the chest-of-drawers
to colour cream with brass handles.

You would wait for a silhouette to fashion
a lamp with a gold fringe; a book alongside.

You would wait for curtains to flower lilac,
for light to seep through linen weave.

You would wait for a chink to streak
down a mirror; a hairbrush would appear.

You would wait for furry caterpillars to flow
as wavy blue lines of candlewick bedspread.

You would stretch out your legs;
soft toys at the foot of the bed would shuffle.

You would wait for first voices in the house.

Tobacco Leaves

Above your childhood bed,
the ceiling slopes to the door
of the loft – small brass latch,
cave-like hollow beyond:

home-grown tobacco leaves
hang along beams to dry
like leathery clothes of the dead;
you dread a gust of wind will fling

the door wide   leathery clothes
flapping, exposing
a rusted metal trunk from the war.
Cousin Paul boasts

he's seen inside:
khaki uniforms   and a dagger!
You will never escape
the stench of mud and blood.

Degas Dancer

When we are really moved at the theatre we are
always both on the stage and in the auditorium.
Roger Fry, *Vision & Design*

Degas dancer turned up in a box of old photos,
silver fish had nibbled holes in the brittle backing.
The glass was cracked.

As a girl, she was unafraid of the dark,
her mother left nightlights along the mantelpiece.
Degas dancer turned...

She traced the grace and sway on the wall,
flames flickered a cinematic haze of gauze skirts.
The glass wasn't cracked.

Prima ballerina (no bit part, no *corps de ballet*),
she stepped, leapt, patterned in a sea of evanescent green.
Degas dancer turned, turned, turned...

Her child body in smooth satin, layers of net
sprinkled with flowers, pointe shoes, ribbon.
The glass was not cracked.

In finale, she slid into a bow of glory, applause,
blur of bouquet; the red rose from a prince
as if glass would never crack.
Degas dancer in box of old photos.

Doll

My sister once cut the hair of a brand new doll;
locks scattered over the eiderdown like when the cat
caught a blackbird. Mum rescued the doll, held it close,

wanting to warm it; the little china head fitted the crook
of her elbow. She stroked the bristly scalp, felt undulat-
ing indentations. So at the bathroom sink, she removed

the dress, tucked the doll beneath her arm, its eyes
rolled back. She dipped nailbrush in soap, scrubbed
the bristly wig until the glue came off. Tugged

the dress back over the head, stiff little arms through
sleeves. Sat her up, arms spread like wings. Sculpted
curls blended with feathered knit of shell-pink dress.

Shoes

Each night, we lined-up school shoes,
big to small, heel to toe
at the scullery door,
brown lace-ups in winter,
sandals with daisy cut-outs in summer.
They waited
patiently as grown-ups in a bus queue
for father to emerge
from behind the *Evening News*.

He spread newspaper on the table,
tin of polish, prized apart the brushes,
one matt, dipped in polish,
he dabbed over scuffed toes.
The other, golden-bristled as a hair brush
to shine with quick sharp strokes.
Then he clapped the brushes together,
prayer-like,
until the following night.

Bognor Regis, 1962

The photo has a lingering animation:
girls in bubble bathers skip in shallow water,
lines of frothy waves frozen in time.

With hair newly bobbed, they trail streamers
of seaweed, free of the weight of wet plaited hair
... animation lingers.

Bright breeze, squawky gulls, reflections squint
glassily back, a new look, a light-headedness,
frozen in time.

His shock, scowl, disappointment,
Mother's sigh, a soft exhalation of breath,
the aftermath lingers:

lowering their eyes, the shame
as he walked away, silent
as frozen waves.

That is when the trio went to the sea,
the girls, their mother somewhere
near. Froth of waves, frozen lines, yet linger-
ing animation rings with laughter.

Dead Bells
(in the grounds of a psychiatric hospital, 1959)

The wood was out of bounds.
Strange people lingered there   and stared.
But Poppy and me   crept out the garden gate
           raced through summer grass
quickly trampling stinging nettles.
           The trees much taller closer-up!
Cow parsley made us sneeze
           we squeezed   through a brambly gap.

In the cavernous wood   sky disappeared.
Moss grew underfoot   the air was dank as mist.
We stopped   and stared:
                     a lake of deep violet-blue.
Trees towered all around
                     dark-coated men   the dead.

A breeze   stirred   the blue.
We stroked a silken surface   smoothed a tepid lake.
Picked a single stem to have a closer look:
           five   frail   pendulous bells.

A hush of insect buzz   leaf rustle.
Sparrows   flitted   strung their words in dares!
We looped our gingham skirts   into apron pockets
           picked the pretty bluebells   irresistibly.

           * * *

Our mother was aghast   at where we'd been
        but   *poor bluebells*   was all she said.
No more than girls like us   turning drab already.

We put fist-fulls of bluebells in jam jars
                for a last drink of water.
At dawn   we stared at the dead.

To the Lake

a path through Michaelmas daisies
a swung-open gate
onto the flagstone pavement
past a blur of semis
Nana's warm hand
navy court shoes, beige stockings
her slow steps
around the corner
a stretch of rhododendrons
white flowers, yellow pollen inside
the fragrance of scent bottles –
you pull her to run   clutching
a paper bag of stale bread
through an archway
gust of wind
oak trees   drifting leaves
then, an opening:
a grassy slope down to the lake
the gliding of swans
scattering of mallards
crumbs on muddy water
the lapping

Triple Mirrors

After you died Nana, I went to your room,
it was dark like that place beneath the breakwater
where barnacles cling and children never dare hide.

I opened a blind, a stuck window, breeze fanned
and fanned the room, light across your dressing-
table, triple mirrors. Amidst perfume bottles,

hairbrush, amber beads, your art deco box,
walnut with inlaid mother-of-pearl; guiltily
as if invading privacy, I lifted the lid,

postcards of seaside scenes, turquoise Quink,
stamps, shells, keys, coins, and with sand-like
grit beneath my nails, I heard an echo of the tide
a slow swish, swish...

I tried a jet-diamante comb in my hair, the mirrors
shimmered silver; as if through mist, your blue-
grey eyes came back, three times, to look at me,
waves swept and swept the shore...
the room so empty without you.

Part Two

At the House where my Father was Born

It hurts to go through walls, it makes you sick,
but it's necessary.
Tomas Tranströmer

I'd expected a labyrinth of small dark rooms, yet
the house was lit marigold, scooped out like a pumpkin for Halloween
Flames flickered and spat in a wide fireplace
   a seaweedy stench had swept in   brushed walls with sea mist
Oak beams as broad as shoulders   seemed safe
        the floor dipped like a ship

There was a tavern of voices outside
     laughter   bickering   sniggering
gossip in the street   lingering Victorian morals
        Crash of sea over rocks   din of death bells
                                          It was 1917

I was through that door   that painting, that wall to god knows where

A Woman in Blue Reading a Letter
        a crinkly unfolding of paper sound
a letter that never came   after the Somme

Her sigh   swish of skirt
     I turned   she passed the mirror   a silvery blur
        a light crunch of shoe on wooden board
     I saw the horror of her unwed shame   in my own face
        the same mirror that once held her

O to curl into the stillness of that blue velvet chair
        its painterly stopping of time
Walls giddied me   terrified me   the emptiness of that room

She was banished
        He grew as his grandma's thirteenth child

          *   *   *

I went through silence   a room bathed with pale sunlight
      It was late afternoon in winter
From a window   across a meadow towards the sea
I saw him walking away
He carried the burden of those walls
on his dark days   dark, dark, days
      Shoulders hunched
      he went towards the sea
                the openness of the sea
                          the sea...

Walls Haunt Me – in two voices

1.

First voice (2014):
Wise as his weathered face,
my father's old oak desk
kept secrets hidden for years,
but now,
in the unfolding of letters,
whispers drift from slant of prose;
and a sepia photograph:
Dot and Marjorie, July 1916.
Dot, my Nana, slightly behind her sister,
in fear, I'm told,
of revealing her unwed shame.

The girls wear identical dresses,
wool fabric hangs from thin shoulders,
drop waists, skirts mid-calf;
arms at the same geometric angle
show symmetry of movement like dancers,
straw hats looped on a fence like hoop-la.
The backdrop, St Martin's Cottage;
windows either side of the door.
You'd never guess the labyrinth of rooms.

A crease down the photo suggests
someone almost tore it in half.
Instead, the photo hidden,
as Dot was hidden.

2.
Dot's voice (August, 1916):
The scullery's thick with steam.
Mother is lifting hot sheets
from the copper;
I push and wind
through the mangle.
Concentrate girl!
Her voice sounds distant;
I'm far away;
time stops like a painting;
I'm looking onto a scene;
it can't be real,
the room's a blur.
I fight a light-headedness,
but fall.
The floor is stone cold;
she's leaning over me,
stroking my forehead;
my body slumped;
my frock tight,
it restricts my breath;
tears leak from my eyes.
I'm sorry Mother, I'm sorry.
She's hitting me,
screeching at me;
the floor's as cold as death;
I'm shivering,
trying to crawl away

but I'm tangled,
my skirt, heavy and
sopping wet from the floor.
Help me!
but she's in a rage,
kneeling;
hands pressed over her eyes;
rocking back and forth.
*That boy... he'll not
come back from the front.*
Such a mess in the scullery
with washing half done.

3.
Dot's voice (a day later):
I'm locked in the middle room;
a window to the stair well;
no daylight.
I'm hidden,
my sisters forbidden anywhere near;
chatter drifts from the kitchen.

Last summer's cotton frock
hangs on the door,
flat as a paper cut-out.
I'm cheap, she said.
Wear this:
a smock of drab cloth;
its weight drags me down;
the rug is threadbare:
strands of blue and red
worn beige
and smooth as string.

In the corner,
a clover-leafed table, where
a school bible was flung
like a bird in flight.
Read it, she said.
I peruse a colour plate
of a shepherd,
lambs in grass

and long for outdoors,
the sky,
to hear birds scavenging
for mulberries
in the tree;
to make daisy chains on the lawn.

Time is slow,
each quarter hour
a *dong, dong,*
grandfather clock in the hall.
I lay on the bed,
rose-patterned wallpaper
smells dusty;
trace spidery cracks on the ceiling;
damp patches change into shapes,
clouds or faces;
cobwebs trail strands of grey hair.

Not think of months ahead, Mother said.

After I give birth, I'll be sent away
    – GIVE BIRTH –
words that have nothing to do with me.

4.
First voice (St Martin's Cottage, 2016):
I pause at the doorway,
your cramped cell, renovated now,
a bath where a bed would've been,
sink squeezed in a corner.
An airless space;
I tremble
as if my body remembers
confinement,
dankness,
the enclosure of walls.

It's hard to imagine
how you filled time:
that bible
splashed and stained
like rash of measles on skin,
fever and delirium,
being quarantined, solitude,
boredom;
did you balance the book on your head?
take three steps
table to door, turn
one, two, three back, turn;
did the bible slip to the floor?
a mess of feathers and broken wing?
Did it splay open
at a colour plate of a shipwreck?

when the ship was caught,
and could not
bear up into the wind,
we let her drive...
Those words, I remember exactly
from the old bible you read to me.

O Nana, were you bullied?
Did she say,
Stick-a-smile-on-your-face-girl,
Did you take courage
and, like a ship at sea,
dip and lurch,
one moment peering
down a stairwell
the next lifting, dragging
covers from tangle of bed;
barely space to stand,
smoothing, tucking sheets, blankets,
sides, top, bottom;
eiderdown flopped on top;
did bits of prickly feather scratch
your arm, your face?

Suddenly I'm out of there!
Down steep steps,
walls haunt me,
enclose me.
I leave part of me behind
as you did, Nana.

O the softness
of your grey wool frock;
we played ludo with bright counters,
and the ritual of making beds,
not knowing then
of this tiny museum,
at the house where my father was born.

A Day in April, 1939

They shut me up in Prose –,
Emily Dickinson

A bunch of daffodils on her lap
like a meagre offering of gold in exchange
for a son   stolen   twenty-one years ago;
lush fields rush past, her reflection in glass
as vague as his knowledge of her.
A man in the carriage has a newspaper:
    WAR, WAR   nothing but war.

The day happens so fast –
from the train, down a lane past the church,
gulls squawk and soar; at the door to St Martin's,
black paint peeling, brass knocker tarnished,
party sounds come from inside – her son's birthday.
The door opens   her brother older, jovial, glass in hand.
Phyllis too   *Dot's here. Dot's come back!*
The family crowd around...
How dare you!   Mother's hair is white.
The daffodils drop to the floor,
Dot steps into the low-beamed room.

Here is her son   Alexander   a stranger
but like in a dream, or a vision, she knows it's him,
tall   solemn   shock of wavy brown hair.
I'm your mother... she blurts;
he retreats, vanishing into shadow of an alcove –
she follows through a maze of dark rooms, fumbling
up wooden stairs   stopping
at the door to the middle room –
horror of memory blackening the moment –

but here he stands   by the window, fresh curtains,
a bed, a bookcase, row of leather bound books.
Alexander...
at the softness of her voice, he turns –
those watery green eyes   break her.

Alexander (late 1939)

The portrait is propped between ticking clock and vase of red-gold chrysanthemums. Light casts sheen on nose, cheek-bones, tip of ear; immaculate teeth, crease either side of the mouth. Dark hair crinkles back from the forehead. The gaze distant. Khaki collar adjusted for the camera, the way a mother checks a child for school, kisses a little boy cheek.

He was her newborn son wrapped in a shawl   she held so briefly   pressing her lips to his downy head.   They took him that awful moment   relived over and over for twenty-one years the emptiness...   Today he's gone again   there's a terrible chill in the house, hollow sound, snow on the ground.

Beneath clock and vase of chrysanthemums, petals and sticky yellow pollen litter the dresser.

In Hilda's Garden

Dot's pale coat is undone, her skirt hangs below showing thin ankles and low worn shoes. Right foot stepping forward like fifth position in ballet, she leans against her son. His shoulder higher than hers; stance solid, prepared for war, but relaxed that day in an open-necked shirt.

Smile please, say cheese   and that's how they remain (April 1939) in Hilda's garden, window in the background, foliage reflected in glass.

Early morning, third of November, the photo arrives by post. Dot doesn't need Hilda's face at the window calling everyone in for tea; electric light in the kitchen; aroma of freshly baked scones; her son's leap of delight. It all floods back. She fits the photo in her purse, snugly, against her identity card.

Night after night, she trudges home in the blackout, gas mask looped over her shoulder, hand clasping the purse. His presence alongside her: steady rhythm of boots, slight whiff of tobacco, teeth lightly crunching his pipe. Sometimes he clears his throat, and she waits...

Swallows

The morning smells of toast –
but the butter knife slips
and stains the cloth.

Toast cools on the plate;
tea in a mug forms a scum;
a wasp fusses over the marmalade jar.

Her serviette falls to the floor.
The washing-machine spins,
and slumps.

No-one comes to the door;
sparrows peck at silver tops on the step.
Front blinds gape open, after dusk.

A passer-by might spot the swallows
swooping and flitting for midges –
cup-shaped nests beneath the eaves.

But only walls know, at nightfall,
swallows squeeze through a skylight, and
circle her empty bed.

Piece of Lace

just a piece of lace she left. a crocheted collar for a neat black dress. reddish-beige. could be blood-stain. imagine a Victorian brooch at her throat. a stab wound a spurt. stubborn stain would remain. women took risks for vanity. steel pins spiked through hats. elastic beneath chins. the ping. the sting. but see the lace her face in the oval mirror. powder-pink. mirror-mirror frail face full of grace. her wrinkled hand winding silk around a crochet hook. one moment stretched smooth as rose petal. then puckered slack. a relaxed slump. her last breath. last click of crochet hook. let her rest in peace forever and ever. scent of lavender drifts with cigarette smoke ashes to ashes... just a piece of lace.

Never Trust Tulips

The room filled with silence,
puce pink tulips bunched together
like oval-faced nurses in a war-time photo;
lanceolate leaves dangled lush as arms,
stems knee deep in a vase of sepia water.

The tulips   watched her drift away –
they did nothing
but inhale oxygen   greedily.

There's no grave-stone   but alongside
the flint wall of a seaside church
within earshot   of choir song and gull call,
amongst pale grass, stray as unplaited hair,
mauve and black anemones sway
on wiry stems.
                It's as if,
she pushes them up with her fingertips
to let us know   she's there.
        She would never trust tulips.

Tulips in Black and White

Sadness overwhelms me in this circle of cut
flowers; some face me, plead for help, but if

I was to cradle one tulip-heavy head in my palm
like a premature baby, would its petals (that remind

me of my mother's skin when she was old) fall
to the floor? Others turn away in a dried blush

of shame. Just a few plump bodies flaunt sheen
on velvet cloaks, yet stems stoop weary.

They wait in colour-obliterated twilight.
Forgotten.

Part Three

Postcard to a Sibling

my love letter to the planet,
Sebastião Salgado,
Genesis, Natural History Museum, 2013

i.
I perused the shimmering images of Salgado,
chiaroscuro palettes of black and white:
penguins   cormorants   whales   sea lions,
volcanoes   the Antarctic   glaciers of Alaska...
afterwards, I chose a postcard of African elephants –
then back home in Australia
I leant it against the photo of my father
and the carved elephants he brought back from war.

ii.
I recalled the house of childhood   the sounds,
back-drop of war –   his portrait on the dresser,
khaki uniform   how the light stroked his brow,
chink of teeth   his smile,
the row of elephants alongside   and, on Sundays:
silver cutlery on crisp white damask,
the meagre roast,
grown-ups' stories of the black-out, ration books,
nurses and hospitals, underground shelters, the blitz,
the silences.

iii.
in winter, we scattered toast crumbs on snow,
then indoors, beneath a table, its folds of dark cloth,
we looked through the cold glass of French doors:
sparrows   blackbirds   specked the whiteness –
the room droned with the voice of BBC news.

iv.
today I will buy a stamp for the postcard,
write nothing but my name –
she will remember.

Because He Tried So Hard

Cold glass against my face,
the train juddered about to leave,
I saw him   tweed jacket   slope of shoulders
I leapt, rushing to him   until I remembered...

The news came by letter,
it said, Dad hadn't got long –
the quiet kitchen   silent phone,
children cheering at sport across the park,
it was night in the UK,
I made cup, after cup, of tea
and went into the rooms of childhood:
his nicotine-stained hands, gold signet ring,
whiskey breath, raspy cough,
deafness   an injury of war,
he could never hear on the phone,

yet, that night   he heard my voice,
Hello sweetie, he said   a miracle
or perhaps because he tried so hard...

He never made it to the phone again.

Not Thinking it would be Forever
(after Dorothy Hewett)

i.
The car slowly moved me away,
you watched from the kitchen window,
quietly   then suddenly pleading.
I play the moment over and over,
wanting to run back   *Mum, I won't go.*

But I let the car take me: a salted road,
snow banked-up either side, ploughing
through a blizzard of tears, wipers
like a metronome clearing half moons,
headlights creating circles of falling snow.

I left,
launching into bright new Februaries,
not thinking it would be forever.

Bush-fires rage here tonight; headlines
on the news read   *Prepare to leave.*
Your face vivid at the kitchen window,
fading.

ii.
Oh Mum! There are photos of you
in best dresses, neat hair, lipstick.
But none of you in your kitchen, floral
wrap-over apron, sleeves pushed-up, pressing
on the rolling pin, stretching-out the pastry;
spirals of apple peelings alongside.

Or, brushing away a strand of hair, flour
smudged across your forehead, cheeks
flushed from heat of the oven.
Or, saying   *Let's have a cuppa*,
tea pot, milk, cups, on red Formica table.
Or, of tapping your fingers impatiently;
raising your chin to the rights of women.
Or, arms folded, gazing out the window
waiting for a pie to bake.
There are no close-ups of your hands.

The Shrine

The day is like a painting   hazy
with sun; our shoes plod and slot
in the grooves of bridle path.
We climb to the Sycamore tree.

Potted petunias clustered beneath,
plastic daffodils stuffed in the earth,
pansies with faces like Pekinese,
a candle in a jar   a teddy bear.

The shrine is for anyone,
a partner, a parent, a child,
even a dog who liked to walk here.

We sit on a wooden bench;
my sister's bracelets   rustle
silver sounds   approximations
of what we might say.

Far away   through fields of long grass,
I spot a girl in a red dress   running away –
I can't tell if it is our mother as a child
or if it is me   running towards her.

Sisters

The promenade is monochrome   We push through sea mist
Poppy was six the year she had TB   Now she asks
what it was like for me   My raincoat clings like dank seaweed
                        my lips part   but don't speak

Outside a shut door   I hear a doctor murmur   sanatorium
Our mother's nurse-voice   No!
We search through blindness   my ring clinks a chrome railing
Old people in parked cars peer through half moons of windscreens
        sip thermos tea   wait for mist to lift
              hush of the shore   sanatorium   sanatorium   No!

Creep away   slink in shadows   corridors   flat against walls
        make myself scarce   I am selfish

                                      Words won't form
A storm has thrashed pebbles across the path   shoes crunch, crunch
We're wrenched apart for a year   no children allowed near
Her room is quiet as daisies in grass   mine is drab   dark
                      a ship's horn sounds through gloom

I search for words
We link arms   a breakwater emerges down the slope of the beach
I delve further into thickness of the past
                    darkness heartens   hearkens
              opens into a softness   the warmth of mauve

An oval mirror veiled with silk   Auntie Phyllis smells of lavender
She lets me play with her silver-backed hairbrush   long black hair
trails down to her waist   it has threads of white   At night
we listen to the swish of the sea   sew sequins on damask

The chalk cliff towers above   craggy and bright
Our mother washes salt-encrusted windows with soapy water
Sunlight seeps into the house at the cliff
Poppy's hair has grown into a cascade of gold
                              Daffodils laughed, I say

After *The Secret Garden*

During the interval of the Haydn choral concert,
my sister (once princess of the dress-up box) said   *Let's go...*
We went down the side of the church,
slipped through a gate –
the brass padlock a fake   for those in the know –
into a flint-walled garden   a kind of overgrown underground.
The light was green.
A soliquacity:
sparrows   finches   coo of wood pigeons,
bees on hives   and cabbage-white butterflies.
Trees   tall as stilts   connected earth to sky,
roots tipped ancient graves   almost merrily.
I craned forward but could not decipher a name.
It was a dead-quiet afternoon.   No traffic.
We looked at each other;
we'd gone back in time, she was nine.   I must call her Mary.
She wore a print frock, green   herring-bone braid around the hem.
Mine, identical in red   familiar   soft lawn against my skin.
Thunder rumbled in the distance   (furniture moved in heaven).
Bees swarmed overhead.
I said I'd read   bees are losing their olfactory sense,
pollution is the problem.
But the information had little application;
we were in a novel   from 1910.
Grasses and buttercups whispered to one other,
the wind puffed at dandelion clocks.
When it was time   for the concert to re-commence,
we trailed back inside,
slid along the pew   waited   in freckled silence.

The Mulberry Tree (circa. 1600)

Beneath the mulberry tree, the ground moved
and I looked up at the dark tangled limbs:
arms and legs of children who'd ever played there.
Mulberries fell about my feet;
my mother's voice intervened   *Mind where you walk*
dog-dirt on the hop-scotch pink pavement
outside our house, the cold lounge, aroma of gin and orange,
roast turkey on Christmas morning. Always at eleven o'clock,
     dong   dong   of the grandfather clock.
Raise your glasses, father would say   *To absent friends!*

Names that followed, gone away, killed in wars.
The carpet with maroon roses, squashed mulberries,
and up above, the grown-ups lifting their warm arms.
     Merry Christmas! Merry Christmas!

Beneath the mulberry tree,
the children who grew up and went away   sang   sang.
     Here we go around the mulberry bush,
     the mulberry bush, the mulberry bush...
Someone offered me a bottle of homemade mulberry wine.
The ground moved.
It does, she said.

Much later, you and I at the table with the wine,
plain label, printed name.
We discussed how to soak it, to save it   forever.
Pulled the cork, poured the wine,
raised our glasses   *To absent friends!*
It tasted awful...

Anemones (black & white)

In the *memento mori*   of the photograph
heliotropic faces of anemones   are raised   adoringly
                  stems clasped in a vase   invisibly.

Prior to the moment   let's call it 8pm   a summer's night.
I watch from the wings
        midnight-blue velvet drapes   along the window ledge
                an oblique angle   twist of the head.

The photographer   on the ceiling   rests
        flat as a bed   peering through the crystal chandelier.
She wears camouflage   shell-pink chiffon   and pearls
      the shadow of the chandelier
                        dapples her with lacy cloth.
It's then.

The wind-flowers flit in   khol-eyed   and wild
      pushing-open French doors
           petalled frocks   from the fairy shop.
They form a corolla   choreography
      for a ballet score   or game of musical chairs
              pirouette
        stop   gaze   at a single spot
     an aureole of wispy foliage   spins around their heads.
A pleasing arrangement   the photographer says
         harmonious hues   a hazy reflection in water.

After the moment   in the stillness
                we fill our arms with flowers.

Above a Seedy Bridal Shop

You never know what to expect   in a holiday let
booked on the internet.
The Dickensian street   had a decadent feel.
Flat two   I found above a seedy bridal shop.
The door was ajar.
A vestibule   whiffed of mothballs and peppermint breath.
Then as I went up the stairs   the air took on a hazy tint.
A glass table   opaque as an iced cake.   Dusty.
A spray of whitish flowers
        anemones   roses   campion   forget-me-nots
stuffed in a vase   as if hurled by a bride   and caught
by a girl with cautious hands.   Then ditched.
A chipped vase had a nipped in waist   laced at the back
        twisted and wrung like a dishcloth   tight as a corset.
Even the spiders had fled.
The ivory clock   had stopped at a twenty to nine.

Despite what the website implied:
a clock wound each Saturday   (on changeover day)
        a barefoot Isadora with flowing dusters
            fresh flowers tied with blue satin ribbons
fluid baroque folds   a möbius strip   the turning of wrists.
And something new   a window view:
        a Rodin replica   *La Cathédrale*   in the street.
A scent of summer flowers lifts skyward   the blurb said
        ethereal   choral voices in a medieval church.
Left in the lurch
that clock too   had stopped at a twenty to nine.

Victorian Ring

O Nana, you trusted me
with your Victorian ring –
row of diamonds glisten-
ing clear as light,
But now, with regret,
I write to confess
how many times I let
nine carat claws snag,
sharp as a cat's,
on my cardigan sleeve.
A diamond is missing –
unlike the cute gap
of a child's lost tooth,
there's a cavity, grim
as a grave.

O Nana,
why am I recalling you,
white permed hair, tucked
into nape of a wing-backed chair
blowing smoke-rings like Daddy;
why do I hear you sing
that light-hearted song:
    Gone forever, lost forever,
    O my darling Clementine
as you did those years ago?
I hardly deserve forgiveness.

Miss Philipou's Class

I travel back and forth through years   different hemispheres.
Poetry began in this little book.
The maroon linen cover faded brick-pink   gold lettering dulled
but clear as Braille to touch   the radiance of everyday words.
Leafy-patterned endpapers   eggshell   speckled with mould,
       Left in the rain.   A blue-inked name.

I turn pages
      Miss Philipou's voice   switches on   like a radio song.
        Narrative Poetry   she cries with darting eyes
pushing-up her black-ribbed sleeves   jingling silver bangles.
We shop in Goblin Market   skip through streets of Hamelin.
      Listen to a wedding speech.   Marvel
at the wingspan of an Albatross.   Repeat the O!
      of The Wraggle Taggle Gypsies O!
Help build a canoe   for Hiawatha's sailing.

We chant by rote: Deirdre alongside   a cast on her arm
scribbled with autographs.   Susan   Beryl   Gina.
Margarita   in pink plastic spectacles   her empty seat
    remedial classes with Sister Bernadette.
Helen went out with a boy   from the Secondary Modern.
But Jane Hallem   her long red hair in front of me
         died in childbirth at just sixteen.
Her mother wore a grey serge coat   pushed a black pram around town.

Sister Anne-Marie

We saw her mopping floors in corridors,
serve at supper table, but never at assembly.
Poor Sister Anne-Marie, tall and stooped
as a lamp-post, habit frayed around the hem,
hair beneath a veil tightly bandaged, and
tortoiseshell spectacles held together with sticky tape.

The day she came to class, girls muffled giggles,
but she brought tales of saints and miracles. Amazed
we gazed at stained glass windows, bible illustrations;
agog at tales of trips to Lourdes, multiplication of fish,
and Moses in the bulrushes.   A black rosary
swung from her belt, how we longed
to finger and whisper the beads.

Only once did I see her in the dormitory at night:
long black hair trailed down her white nightgown,
saint-like   ordinary.

Marilla

It was ten years since school, that day
we met on the high street. Same blue eyes
quick with laughter; your face pale and oval
as a nun's beneath a hand-knitted beanie.

Your heart, *a year at the most*, you said
reaching out to comfort me, insisting you'd
had a good life. I recalled the crystal rosary,
silver crucifix in your school-skirt pocket.

The memory mixes with playground sounds,
flaxen plaits, creak of desk lids, pens dipped
in ink wells, earthy smell of exercise books,
the secret notes we wrote in class.

The news arrived today: your sister wound
wool around the needle for the last time.

The Boy from the Grammar School

Act one:
The day I turned fourteen   eye-level with the mirror
and boys   I locked the bathroom door,
tried a little hair lightener
on my fringe   gingerly at first   then
tipped it   all over my head   it fizzed and stung
fifteen minutes   for maximum effect.

My father called it   *Barmaid blonde!*
My mother said   *The nuns at school must never know.*
She took me to Annette's   perms, shampoos and sets.
Dye it brown, she said   and left.
I asked Annette   for *Black!*

Act two:
An underground coffee bar in town   banned
for convent girls, but
Maeve and me   checked the street   down shady stairs
     a cavernous space   dimly lit   crimson walls.
We ordered cokes   a corner table.
The boy from the Grammar School   collar turned up,
fed coins into the jukebox   the Crystals sang
          Well he walked up to me
          and he asked if I wanted to dance...
He glanced over   didn't recognise me at first
but when I whispered his name
he said, *I like your black hair.*
The song hung in the air:
          And then he kissed me
          And then he kissed me...

Three Pictures

i.
From an open window,
I watch my teenage sister:
pastel twin set, pleated skirt, skinny legs
scuttling away,
small suitcase bumping her thigh.
The street narrows in the distance,
she becomes smaller, fainter   gone.

ii.
A doorway frames her quiet room;
stillness cloaks me;
flatness of blue candlewick bedspread,
empty slippers beneath
– leopard spots, wedge heel –
her clip-clop sound.
A china doll on a chair   stares blankly,
black lashes;
a sparrow flits past the window.
I sift through her record collection,
borrow a Beatles LP –
a melancholy song   *She's leaving home...*

iii.
In a photo of the day she returns
– Afghan coat and Indian hippy skirt –
I hear the sound of Joan Baez
playing   over and over
on a new red Dansette.
Dad says it sounds like moaning
and   *Whatever are the words?*

An Attic Window (Montmartre)

11pm: a midsummer Saturday night.
It was a giddying height above the hub-bub   the whooping it up
        shrieks   laughter   along the *Place du Théâtre*.
In a café   with an olive green awning   an accordion played Piaf.

A dog yapped on a wrought-iron balcony   a flame geranium.
Shutters flung open like an advent calendar   a lamp or two
        a room lined with books   a woman poured a glass of wine.
I pondered a rear window line for this poem   a cinematography
but a child wandered onto a balcony.
I couldn't look.   A cobbled street below.
I turned from the window   the ceiling sloped to the floor.
I heard motor-bikes roar   revelry   the night punctured with sirens.

In a dream I recalled   a box-brownie photo   me beside a swing
        three badges pinned   proudly   to my school blazer lapel.
I thought I was tall   but I was small
            blue ribbons   on my tight plaits   flew back.
I swung high   and dropped   from a starless sky.

            * * *

I had no idea   how melancholy   the morning would be.
        I thought of the day after Septimus fell.
Trees scattered leaves in the square   a deserted theatre door
        a closed boulangerie   tiny boutique   a silent school.
Shopkeepers swept rubbish   hosed pavements
                       rivulets ran down gutters.
I climbed steep steps in shadow of the *Sacré Coeur Basilica*.
        The bells dong   donged   and swelled...

Rural Normandy

We took a photo on arrival:
stone cottage with a well out the front,
and then stepped off camera,
into low-ceilinged rooms,
windows with red gingham curtains;
a ladder to a hayloft
where our children would sleep
but they crept into our big old bed,
the five of us together.
Then at dawn, a peasant woman,
horse 'n' cart, black frock and clogs,
Bonjour Madame, mes enfants, she called
and memory's cinematography opens
onto an expanse of verdant fields,
the children laughing, chasing
after the cart – returning with bowls
of milk, warm from the cow,
smiles wide as clowns.

Only once we drove to town,
a narrow winding lane –
the green mini sped past,
hit a tree,
just a boy   eyes wide open.

If only to go back
to the moment of the photo.

Part Four

Surely Someone
'Tenement Building' (black & white photograph)
Chris Kilip, Tate Britain, 2014

you view the house from across the street
part of a terrace   it fills the frame
the roof is cut off   no sky   dim light

upstairs   a balcony
door   window   bricked-up   defiant
downstairs   a curtain is torn
you move in closer   but can't see into the room
front door   pint of milk on the step
dustbin on the kerb

it's the pint of milk that disturbs you
you wait   if you wait   surely someone
will fetch in the milk...

not even a sparrow pecks at the silver-top
the house   bereft of sound
is like the backdrop to a disused stage
rain has left sheen on the tarmac

a month later   you read:
bull-dozers arrived   like thunder

No-one Knew

On platform twelve, a group was gathering
around a long-limbed youth;   sat on a cold
metal bench, he leaned to one side suspended
in space like a puppet   waiting for a train,
    waiting –

his eyes were open aquamarine,
pale skin stretched like a caul over porcelain;
blue lips etched peace, oblivious
to the thud, the beat, resonating
from an i-pod dropped
alongside his still shoe.

A woman lurched forward, wanting
to hold him, warm him, but the guards
pulled her away.   *Move along, move along.*
No-one knew how he came to be there –
t-shirt immaculate,
freshly laundered jeans.

Passengers crammed into carriages – faces
slid away shocked as dolls in a cupboard.

A siren grew louder, louder   then stopped.

Für Das Kind

Kindertransport Memorial
by Flor Kent, Liverpool Street Station

Amidst the bustle, there is stillness   silence:
a girl, a boy, a suitcase, sculpted in bronze.
The girl stands on a stone plinth,
sturdy legs, arms hanging by her sides.
She has nothing, no-one left.
There are dark lines beneath her eyes, and
she stares as if horror is trapped in her skull.
The boy sits on the edge of the plinth;
he's been put there, put off a train.

Orphaned.

They are drenched in sepia;
the suitcase fills the space between them.

A temporary fence encircles the exhibit
like a flimsy cage; a thin crowd has gathered
but a man with an empathetic face,
steps aside for me to read the brass plaque:

In tribute to all those who helped rescue
10,000 Jewish and other children escaping
Nazi persecution...

The desolation of arrival,
sacred in bronze.

London, 1975

You were telling me about your daughter in London
    when I remembered. A drowsy afternoon
    in the office, sleet drifted past the window,
    traffic hissed and purred below.

A bomb exploded, shattered a window. A girl
    called Jill cut her arm, blood seeped
    through her cardigan sleeve, she tied
    a blue silk scarf around the wound.

We grabbed bags and coats, clambered
    down stairs to the street, alarms rang
    in department stores and people poured
    from doors like gravy from jugs.

Tourists, shoppers, workers ran with coats undone,
    the crowd raced towards Oxford Circus
    but barricades, an explosion underground.
    We turned and surged back...

At Selfridges, a mannequin in a crimson frock
    toppled over, dived head-first through
    glass, legs stick-straight in the air,
    a black wig swung like a spider from a web.

Traffic stopped, power cuts plunged us in darkness;
    we lost each other, I almost tripped over
    a man sprawled on the ground,
    a sticky dark halo spread around his head.

Ambulances wailed, screeched up Park Lane,
    around Marble Arch. Louder! Louder!
    Then silence as paramedics swarmed
    over the injured, the lost limbs...

I remember the rhythm of the slow walk home;
    feathery snow-flakes melted
    as they touched the wet tarmac,
    but much is mixed up in my mind.

Bomb scares, alarm bells, media reports;
    a woman threw herself over a child,
    he emerged from her coat unscathed
    like a chick hatched from an egg.

Yet the fear remains, of bags abandoned in shops.
    I wish I hadn't told you about that.

Apartment in Amsterdam

Trees glint alongside the canal,
but following written directions
you turn into a terraced street,
lug a suitcase up flights of steep stairs.
A black door
leads into the gloom of a room.
Flicking the switch of a rickety lamp
throws light on wood floor, dust-brown rug;
sparse furniture is nondescript.
The small window reveals
a vertiginous drop,
dungeon of a courtyard below.
No fire escape.

You are free to leave,

but in 1942, not far from here,
Anne Frank climbed similar stairs.
No suitcase,
a heavy coat over layers of clothes,
the tightness,
a cupboard slid over the door,
claustrophobic,
for months
the hunger,
acrid stench of pickled kale,
no daylight, no daytime sound,
the fear of making sound,
and being found.
Being found.

Bony Fingers

The night I arrived, I smelt white lilies,
studied mismatched architraves, counting
twenty gilt-framed portraits on walls a metre thick.

As the ceiling-rose began to fade, waves grew
loud outside, rustlings came from within walls;
a distinct whiff of white lilies.

They opened little doors, crept out to float about,
swirled above my head.
The frames gaped like an advent calendar.

Bony fingers fiddled with curtains, rattled at latches,
cobwebby frocks, smocks, squeezed through gaps.
All night, I smelt white lilies.

They'd gone to dance along the shore.
At dawn, I heard each frame click shut;
twenty portraits returned.

They'd melted back in musty vaults,
hands crossed over their chests.
A smell of white lilies lingered, lingered.

Dressing Gown

surfing on my i-pad late last night,
i came across an image of a dressing gown,
fine white linen with pastel spots stuck-on:

mandala swirls   catherine wheels,
flying saucers from a sweet shop,
melt-in-the-mouth communion wafers,
a zing of lemon sherbet!

the texture of the cloth crisp as net,
yet soft as home-made paper, rolled thin,
i zoomed-in:

noticed the weave   imagined a loom,
the way a spool dips in-out-in-out-across
and pulls through
like wool,
the way Nana darned stockings
in cross-hatched little patches

i contemplated purchasing
the dressing gown, attempted to resist,
but my face

took its place on screen,
my arms slipped through silken sleeves,
small feet appeared beneath the hem

Alice

after *Triptych Alice* (1957), Charles Blackman

A cat miaows like the screech
of underground train   walls rush
past   then, a door

into a painting of salt-water blue
Alice, flat as Queen of Hearts   wears
schoolmarm blue   blond hair blunted

She stumbles, blind and old   trip-
ping   spilling cups of tea   Daisies
off-their-heads   make terrible mess
    a tipped-up gold-fish bowl
Rabbit (upside-down)   peers
through misty glass   to witness
a crowd   gawping at a magic trick:

Alice in the box   spliced thrice
    –Alice-Barbara-Alice–
she's old, young   tall, small
    Wake up Alice!

A Photographic Portrait
Lauren [Eyes closed], Petrina Hicks, 2003

you are as quiet as a headstone
a choreograph of stillness
fine-chiselled bones
a sculpted masterpiece

your skin is pure   poured-
cream from the milk
your hair vanilla-pale
& as straight as wax tapers

your eyebrows are powdered
expressionless   white as a wig
your eyelids sealed
with bleach-feathered lashes

your ear – a synthetic shell –
mourns the sound of the sea
your lips naked
with the sorrow

you are stillborn
you are a doll
muffled with melancholy
you are ivory

you are stolen   oh where
where are you Lauren –
how long have you been
locked in this blank asylum?

Doris Lessing, 1959

there she is
pensive
shirt-waister frock

i cast my eye
faded paper-backs
intricate
i touch a spine
parched pages
ochred
the mustiness
other people's houses

i am immersed
(vivid
bravery of women
the era

yet surely this photo
unless

fag in hand
dark bobbed hair
crimplene

along a shelf
titles
as vertebrae
take a book
crack open
dusty
of vintage shops
last night's cooking smells

in dystopian tales
as yesterday)
in science fiction
of golden notebooks

is incomplete

she is about to speak

Girl at Bus Stop

a soft Irish voice at my shoulder
pleads *money for a hostel for the night*?
blue eyes   honest as mirrors
dark fringe   pale skin
she wears a cream lace dress
bare shoulders frail as egg-shell
I offer coins from my pocket
her hand is quick
puffy fingers   nicotine-stained
grime beneath the nails –
she vanishes

I take her face aboard the bus to Dublin airport
through the grey of suburbs
see her tucked in a warm bed   soft blanket –
rain slides down the glass
glazes over   opaque as ice
I see her crouched in a corner   cold concrete
floor of a squat   I want to put my cardigan
around her   empty my purse

she'll be there the following night
at the bus station   beside automatic doors
smoking   watching   waiting –
she'll slip off her coat…

Poet on Train

out the corner of my eye, an olive-skinned hand, black notebook on lap. profile in glass like a ruffled blackbird. unclasps a green purse, takes grey-marbled pen, gold nib, writes in black ink. a mark on the back of her hand, could be a mole or an age-spot. too young for an age-spot. an intelligent hand, rounded nails. might be a burn. I see steam billowing from a kettle, hear a screech. someone coaxing her to a tap. but the writing is bold, she'd live alone. no rings, not fuss, get the first-aid kit. she's counting, fingers perfect as piano keys. what does she do? can't be much, jeans, scuffed burgundy ballet shoes. crosses legs, fake tan. deep in thought, jots down a word or two. checks phone, applies scarlet lipstick (using phone for a mirror). stands, is tall. reminds me of a suffragette, must be the black velvet jacket. alights from train, melts into crowd.

Well-thumbed Corner

try different angles [angels merely flit about]. the view from sofa one through an open door: [unlike matisse] a poorly lit ante-room. from sofa two [through tangle of table and chair legs]: white kitchen cabinets, and number 24 on the floor in a well-thumbed corner, dead as a spider. you stand for a semi-aerial view: bali table-runner, wooden fruit bowl, apples, oranges, dark globe grapes, and a dish of roses chocolates. twisting open tinsel wrappers, you reminisce childhood winters by the golden glow of a roaring fire. nana making wine flutes from tinsel paper. a clock on the wall chimes nine. so biding time with a glass of wine, you wander lonely as... barefoot on polished concrete [cold] get distracted by cartoon-style images on how to keep a spotless floor: bucket, white-wig-mop, suds, sloshing washing... eventually you kneel [not unlike star gazing but upside-down] for a myopic study of each tiny fleck and grain.

On (mis)remembering a Bill Viola video installation

The Mermaids in the Basement
Came out to look at me –,
Emily Dickinson

An oneiric dimension to the darkened room,
slight vertigo;
a screen on the wall flickers a sixties tv,
clearing flat grey, and backlit;
sliding-in reveals a gritty texture of sand,
a wave washes and recedes,
pebbles revealed;
you lose the firmness of wood floor
and squelch forward on wet sand;
all is rolling towards you,
pebbles grow big as boulders, granite,
quartz, rough to touch elephant rocks,
but your head is pulled forward as if on a string,
your arms spread like wings,
your feet fly back like a tail;
white and glossy as a gull, feathers flattened
you stream into incoming breeze,
terror drums your ears;
you focus on a circle of light,
it swells and diminishes
leaving water all around
and above;
you are swallowed
engulfed in grey-green, diving for a fish
 – fade out – .

Jetlag at the Kelvingrove

We chose plush velvet seats   front row;
an impromptu decision
to attend an organ recital –
a pleasant sojourn
from tour of museum.
The organist played Bach,
music expanding   exhilaratingly loud.
I studied rafters intricately carved
and longed to sing out loud –
we sang *Frère Jacques* at convent school:
mouths opening, shutting, opening, shutting.
Girls faces swam around me like masks,
a navy gymslip prickled my skin,
starched Peter Pan collar;
mouths opening, shutting, opening, shutting.
Warmth of school-dinners drifted in,
lured me
to a surreptitious nap.
I ignored the final applause.
The organist bowed;
his reprimanding glare   stung
like the eyes of a strict nun.

Merchant Hall (York)

You're in a cavernous hall. All wood.
The floor slopes away   a hint of daylight;
sun is trying to squeeze in leadlight windows
but old glass is thick.
Somewhere up in the beams are murmurs.
You spread around oak-panelled walls
sensing a presence of the dead (proof is found
in framed notices, ochred paper, lists of names).
They're over there   sat in rows on chairs:
men in buttoned velvet coats, hats on laps,
women in feathered hats holding folded parasols.
Ignore them.
You're attracted to a corner with an open fire.
Warm your hands. Discover a long low evidence chest:
1340s, for valuables – easy to carry out in case of fire.
Creak of wooden floor   the chest lifts and shifts;
many hand-sewn leather shoes beneath
like shuffling coffin bearers.
A rattle of valuables   imagine
silver goblets, gold rings, emeralds, rubies,
ropes of pearls, tangled and sparkling.
A woman's scarlet skirt brushes the floor,
a tide-line of dried mud along the hem.
Lift and clonk of a latch –
a tall door gapes open   tourists chatter
into the hall, and   obliterate the past.

Monet's Room
Musée de L'Orangerie

Please enter quietly   it says
The room is oval and white
azure paintings stretch

        around walls   my eyes spread
        over their skin   There is water
        only water   sky and cloud reflect

in opaline light   foliage of willow
drapes shadow   cat paws of breeze
claw the surface   I press my face

        into its sound   Children
        tadpole on the floor   sandalled
        feet waggling   yellow-blue

crayons squeak across paper
a woolly-headed boy bops up
shows teacher his drawing

        I inhale coolness   tendrils
        of pond weed slip down
        my throat

              Drowning is wonderful

Mona Lisa

The sheep are grazing on the Downs;
one stops   for me to photograph it.
Close up   an earthy smell of dung,
and black eyes stare at me   alert.
It turns with a quick skip and trots off:
a woolly behind on deft hoofed feet.
Cumulus cloud drifts over distant hills,
a steep descent to patchwork fields, and
a ribbon of river to the coast.   Sudden
breeze brings an autumn nip to the air...

Eons later   I find the image on my phone:
a sheep with glass-black eyes
how an Italian might paint;
three-quarter profile, upright pose, ample bodied.
The eyes lock my focus,
but the background is blurred like mizzling,
the day has dropped
from my mind   I am mesmerised
by the otherworldly gaze
of glass-black eyes.

Part Five

Sea Houses

The eternal note of sadness in, Mathew Arnold

Sometimes at night I lay awake and listen
to the repetitious hush of the waves, and wonder
how we came to be here, so far from home.

Poppy's house faces the sea, blindly
in northern winter, a silent melancholy indoors:
salt crystallises on windows and vases stand empty
on the ledge, save for sprigs of colourless catkin.

Yet, one day in late June, strolling down the lane,
flowers sprouted through fences and I found
a bucketful of bright Marigolds for sale.
I chose a fist-size bunch tied with string
and wrapped a piece of brown tissue around,
clonking coins into a tin.   With joy
I took the Marigolds to Poppy and she said
O I so wanted flowers for the window ledge.

Tonight I listen to the waves, imagine her
by an open window watching over the sea,
the glow of Marigold beneath her chin
like our childhood game of buttercups;
and with the ebb and flow of thought
I connect to home.

A Black Swan

Strange how she turned up that day

as if I'd put an ad in the local rag for a guardian angel.

Selection criteria: kind heart; must appear when needed...

around the inlet sunlight glittered through wintery plane trees and shimmered over mauve-brown water / she spotted us sped towards us smooth as a skater faster and faster all black and red and dignified a trail of v's widening in her wake she swerved to stop near the shore her neck as slim as a reed arched celestial / an old Labrador stopped in surprise a small wave lapped our shoes / she lifted her brown-black wings spread her quills and revealed a cloud of white plumage beneath

She fitted the job description, exactly!

Imagine the softness beneath the wings of a swan,

how safe it would feel to tuck your toes and fingers into her fine black feathers

and dream of the warmth of the sun.

Ward One, Shenton Park
(an Aboriginal youth, 1995)

Each day I linger at the glass-
walled room   the stillness.
Stillness observed by a nurse;
they watch around the clock
for a sign: a flicker, a twitch.
The shock of dark hair
on the pillow, arch of brow;
quiet face   sunk
deep beneath silent lids –
eyes like a tannin-stained river;
he was swept away,
held under   gasping for breath,
dashed over rocks,
stranded on a white island.
My feet won't move –
foliage brushes the window,
shoes squeak in the corridor,
a tea trolley rattles past.
I want to lean near, to hear the slow
breath, to rest my palm on his chest,
to feel the faint rise and fall.
Thin arms;
the nurse reaches for his hand,
I'm here, I'm here –
gentle waves lap at the shore
coaxing him   to wake.

Age Sixteen

dawn sliced open   with a scalpel
stark   cold   and still
i could not   believe   in the normality of trees
                  birds sang string thin

i drove in the rain: neurological terms   churning
in my brain   my gut   ask the mother   measure
the head   twitch in the eye   get her quick
                  sign here   here

your shaved head   nil by mouth   i could not
tell you   how afraid i was   speed of surgical
gown   clatter   of metal on trays   brisk nurses swished
a curtain   around your bed

                  in the void   i smoothed
a mask of calm on my face   told you stories   of when
you were little   i tried so hard to fold you
                  back into the past
but they came   took you   the length of corridors   i ran
alongside   caught a glimpse of white light
        and the doors swung shut   and

        i stood   with every precious second of you
pressed firmly against my heart
                  for hours   and hours

they brought you back   a bald old man   sunk in white linen
    tubes   drips   oxygen

        the shock of ad hoc   medical remedies
                               the kindness of nurses
      midnight ticked   into the deepest dark
then
as if through the chill of snow
you spoke   like the first purple crocus of spring

Orphan's Boot
(found in rubble beneath a church – New Norcia)

Distempered walls crowd-in cold at the old
schoolroom, resonant with the chant of times
tables, scrape of chalk on slate; a nun might
have leant over a child, white dust on her cuff.

This afternoon, light from a slit window catches
a silver crucifix and reflects onto the dome
of glass cabinet, like sunlight over water.
The exhibit: a small suede boot, without laces.

I sense the vitality of a diminutive foot –
slip my hand into dusty suede and press
tips of my fingers into indents of toes.
I want so much to believe
the child's foot pulled from the trapped shoe
                        and ran and ran...

The Pain of Faces

babies three pieces,
David Cerný
Sculpture by the Sea (2015), Cottesloe

Forget fibreglass and steel   the babies
are flesh and bone of mammoth proportion
Plump shoulders   hefty haunches
sturdy legs   feet, toes
detailed as a Rodin

Splayed fingers   for a slow-limbed crawl
the lift of alternate   hand   knee   hand
neat and purposeful as an elephant

Puckered bar-code faces
a grotesque swipe-and-buy   to be gawped at
Feared!
Why the cruel disfigurement?
This is not the work of a measly god
a mishap   a monster

Then a belt is slung beneath each belly
babies raised high   higher   slight sway
swing overhead   lowered   plumfffed
onto a lorry   flattening of tyres
grooves left in the grass
The artwork lives on   in absence
in the pain of faces.

Famine

bronze sculptures
Rowan Gillespie
Custom House Quay, Dublin.

        Along the banks of the Liffey
the air is saline   a bitter wind cuts from the sea
Skeletal figures   tall marionettes   shuffle
towards an emigration ship

        Clad in rags and grime of disease
a woman clutches a bundle of meagre belongings
like a dead baby   A man has a child   slumped
on his shoulders

        Gaunt faces are open-mouthed
toothless   cadaverous masks   A dull moan
emanates from each exhaled breath   hollow
of skull   Fear of death rattle   haunts
A dog   mangy and lame   stalks them

Decisively

A small figure with orange hair toddles
down the bank. Her father kneels, trusting
her not to step further. He's taking a photo
of mallards resting amongst the reeds.

A shriek of delight! The ducks raise
their heads and glide towards the child –
denim dungarees and red wellie boots.

She throws fistfuls of bread over muggy
brown water, ducks peck and dip, flapping
marbled wings, squabbling, quacking.

Pigeons gather behind her on the grass –
hand on hip like an old woman, she swivels,
quizzical, hair like marmalade rind.   Then,

decisively   she drops bits of bread
on the ground – excited stamping of feet –
ducks waddle onto the grass. She squats
and offers the last scrap from her palm.

Man with Dog on a Bench
(The Rocks, Sydney)

The man looks at me warily;
it's his red-rimmed grey eyes.
The elderly often sit on benches
alone as a single star at twilight.

Yet, in that split second,
I see a glint of silver scissors.
The man's mauve-weathered hand
poised over a miniature black poodle.

His other hand holds the dog close.
Nothing will persuade me to forget
the tilt of the dog's head;
the perplexity in its agate eyes.

Nothing will persuade me to forget
the way the man studies the dog's face;
trims gluey tufts from around its mouth;
cuts the wool from its back.

Clippings fall about the dog's feet;
it steps out of them like clothes.

The man puts on his cloth cap,
hobbles down the cobbled street;
the diminutive dog trots alongside.

The man and dog happy as a film ending
fade into sandstone rock.

The Cat in the Courtyard

on this mild November night
light blares from an open door
disturbing the darkness
rich browns & ochres emerge
reminiscent of a Baroque painting
Rembrandt   Velazquez

a seal point Siamese sleeps
splayed over warm brick tiles
light catches the cream tones
beneath his chin   delicate throat

stone walls blur the background
a Jacaranda tree glints star-kissed
by the deep violet night sky
blossom laden branches gesture
like the gentle arms of a mother
watching over a newborn
in the silence
a figure creeps forward
to stroke the sleek fur of the cat
to feel the knobbly spine

Following, Watching

At night along the terrace:
silver drizzle beneath street lamps,
bright chatter of cafés, cars swish past.
A young couple overtake:
he in skinny jeans, sleek pony tail,
she in gossamer pantaloons, tendrils
of pale hair trail her shoulders. I follow
walking faster away from the cafés;
he leaps onto a wall, a lithe
tightrope walker, arms like wings.
She reaches to steady him, perhaps practising
for a circus. Enthralled, following, watching,
I trip on a kerb, fall flat!

Electric-yellow flashes through my eyelids,
dulls red-mauve and slumps into darkness.
    Can we help you?
Their faces float above like angels.

Cabbage White

you hopped on at the lights   mistook
a parking ticket for a flower –
fairy wings wavered
prettily   on the windscreen –
I drove slowly for you little passenger
you clung to the wiper

but when we stopped
you rocketed up   in shock
           then dropped
                    in freefall
a parachutist's silk
           draped across tarmac

Gone

On a real-estate site, I find photos
of the house where we lived, front door,
red step I bumped the pram over, day after
day. Down the hallway, hollow as a tunnel,
kitchen, bathroom, stark white, chrome,
no kids paintings on the fridge, no ducks
or colourful cups around the bath; yet

leaves of the Silver Birch still quiver
at windows. Into the sitting room, oak
boards stretch across an empty floor. Gone
is the carpet where children played. Gone
are the toy cars, toast crumbs, Lego...

like lifting a stone in the garden,
that space after woodlice have scattered.

Kaleidoscopic Pages

Mention the eighties and I tumble
back to book club, first mortgage, and you
a healthy infant outgrew first *Babygros*.

Your father trudged through snow to a jumble sale,
returned with a bundle of clothes. Distraught,
I couldn't look. That was the frugal eighties.

We'll launder them, he said, also producing
seven vintage Virginia Woolf novels!
all because you outgrew baby clothes.

The washing-machine turned, turned, iridescent
blue, red, yellow, spangled colours of Woolf's
words. Tiny clothes tumble dried, until

each garment smelt as fresh as apple trees.
I slipped a baby suit over your head, played peek-
a-boo with you, pink cheeked, healthy infant.

You studied a lime-green sleeve, mesmerised
as I with colour, turning Woolf's kaleidoscopic
pages; you were a strong healthy infant.
I tumble back, over and over...

An Old Map

find a red sign for railway station:
arrive on a blustery pavement,
air thick with brine   shriek of gulls,
drift down Dean Road like Google Street View,
crossroads   cars   taxis
a striped crossing   a newsagent

from there trace print of street names, blindly
until   Albany Road   Mum's voice
Southdown   Salisbury   Corsica Road
her tone high   or low
where she'd like to live   not live

... at Church Street   you trail
your gloved hand along a flint wall
the smoothness of cut stone   marbled sheen,
rough edges snag the wool of your glove,
Mum's basket looped on your arm –
here is a glass door   it sticks   dings
as you enter   stench of raw meat
you shuffle sawdust with your shoes
and wait in the queue...

Tops of Norfolk Pines

Today, across the park,
the sky is wide open azure,
mares' tails drift white and feathery.
Always, it's the swish of the shore that draws me,
connects me to a place beyond the horizon...

There was once,
a six-year-old me with camera,
climbing steep grey shingle
towards two striped deck-chairs
in a sunny spot beneath a cold sea wall,
the V of her frock, pearls at her throat,
a click sound, the way he bit his pipe,
long socks to his knees,
her floral skirt falling in folds at her ankles,
white sandals, bag with brass clasp –
a memory I never quite reach.

Yet, back across the grass,
I raise my face to the sun:
starry tops of Norfolk Pines are stencilled,
so perfectly, on azure.
It's then she walks alongside,
her laughter bright and yellow as sunflowers.
How she would have loved it here.

Eden Way

At the corner, past the pub,
grainy texture of a fence is uncannily familiar,
the houses whiter than I remember,
the street leafier, prettier...

A kind of blurring
like fanning through pages of an old book:
the smog is thick
Poppy clutches the belt of my gabardine coat
we are feeling our way to school, blindly
along the fence   void of an open gate
occasional headlights creep past.

Ant is pressing me to continue,
       this is it   160!
A skip piled with rubble out front,
the triangular leadlight window is missing.
I wander down the driveway,
a dog barks, and a woman demands
to know...
I stutter about... *my childhood home.*
Oh, she says, from the window of a car.
The street is deserted.
I tell Ant about squeaky brown lino in the hall,
red tiles on the kitchen floor,
              damp washing overhead,

but I don't tell him, that momentarily
she's here beside me   the big pram
her cotton-gloved hand.

Velvety moss grows between lines in the pavement.

Alistair
(for my mother)

we travel through summer rain
train windows framed
with grime – fields glisten –
your dress is pale-blue linen
I lean against your softness

there's a graveyard
overgrown with tall white weeds
you sit forward – searching
long grass dotted
with poppy

a row of miniature headstones
tilt over graves
small as shoe-boxes
engravings smudged with soot
half-hidden with emerald lichen
raindrops slither down glass
like balls of mercury

I held him, you say
and for the briefest moment
you let me into the stillness
of your eyes

I held him, echoes
over and over

Baby Dress

Watery sun from a skylight directs
me to a drawing on the gallery wall.
Baby dress: graphite on white –
bodice, trail of skirt, texture of crinkled net,
lace overlay; the sketch, the scrawl of pencil,
intricate strokes, curls soft as wood shavings.
In the silence, a desire to touch, to hold.

The body remembers warmth, scent of milk.
I hold the softness of cloth, baby garments kept
for years, worn thin as gauze: tiny fingers, fragility
of limbs, skin against skin, hollow of nape, fontanel,
flicker of lashes in sleep, the rhythm of rocking.

Rough surface of paper, fingertips tracing, smoothing, smudging soft pencil lines, blurring, recalling.

First Steps
for SG

You were fourteen months that Christmas,
I knelt (with camera, I'm sure) on the floor by the tree.
You stood little more than a metre away   clutching
a low table to balance   happily tapping, stacking
colourful plastic cups.
I called your name, you turned   stepped
        one   two   three
        hands splayed   wide-gait
        blue velveteen dungarees.
A serendipitous moment
      – milk-teeth and poppy-red cheeks –
                        caught on camera!

or so I thought.
Now, twenty years later, I turn pages of an album
study photo after photo   *à la recherche du temps perdu*,
find your face in profile   my arms outstretched
ready to catch –
            it was not me with the camera at all.
But I recall the amber Pears smell of your hair,
warmth of velveteen in my arms.

Slow Walk Home

Lucas, age three, studies
detail on the pavement: stone
sweet-wrapper, weeds, and now
a wild poppy sprouts through a fence.
He stoops to smell it, as if
it might be perfumed like a rose.

We stare into its black centre:
a fifties London street, November, foggy.
I delve into a tray of scarlet poppies,
not play　　*choose one*　　drop pennies in a tin,
not stare　　at the man in the black leather helmet,
the war　　shrapnel...
Wellie boots chafe welts in the backs of my knees.

We stroll in the warmth of southern sun,
I will boil an egg for his lunch,
teach him to tap-tap, open the top with a teaspoon,
butter bread, cut it into 'soldiers'
to dip in the yolk.
That he never need know about war.

Acknowledgements

Some of the poems have previously appeared in the following publications: *Australian Book Review* 'States of Poetry (WA)', *Axon: Creative Explorations, Black & White Photography, Breath of the Sea, Cordite Poetry Review, Envoi, Rabbit Poetry, Creatrix, dotdotdash, fourW, Jukebox, Positive Words, Poetry and Place Anthology, Poetry d'Amour, Poetic Visions AGWA, Recoil, Unbroken Journal, Westerly, Short and Twisted, Sotto, The Best Australian Poems 2014, The Mozzie, Uneven Floor, Writ Poetry Review*.

My thanks to the following for their support and encouragement: Lucy Dougan, Julie Watts, Dick Alderson, Jan Napier, Reneé Pettitt-Schipp, Ross Jackson, Christopher Konrad, Josephine Clarke, Susan Midalia, Kevin Gillam, Shane McCauley and the OOTA poets. A special thank you to Elizabeth Roberts for the photographs. And to Tony Abbs for being there, always.

Sincere gratitude to Terri-ann White and the UWA Publishing team.

www.ingramcontent.com/pod-product-compliance
Lightning Source LLC
Chambersburg PA
CBHW032232080426
42735CB00008B/819